DIETMAR HÖLSCHER

I0462830

Digitalization
is not a project

Why digitalization projects fail and what are the

ways to avoid it?

A guide for managing directors, stakeholders,

buyers, project managers, consultants and

product owners

2nd iteration 09.2019

© 2019 Dietmar Hölscher

Publisher: firestarter.business

ISBN: 9781082061899

ASIN: B07XTMN2BD

A project is generally defined by various criteria such as:

1. The aim is to create something new that does not yet exist in the desired form.
2. They are limited in time, which means that both the beginning and the end are defined in terms of dates.
3. Projects are unique.
4. Projects are equipped with limited resources.
5. Projects pursue a clearly specified and positively formulated goal.

However, at least 3 of the 5 criteria of a project that are regarded here as general and binding prevent successful digitalization projects.

3

In this book, I discuss the individual reasons why projects are not and cannot be the right choice for digitalization purposes, and I prove this with well-founded scientific figures.

But I am also pointing out alternatives with which it is possible to push ahead with digitalization in one's own company at very low risk, quickly and cheaply.

The way of thinking, one would or could have to convert everything into existing and for other fields established procedures like PRINCE, PMI, PMBoK, etc. on a completely different world, namely that of the digitization sounds tempting, is however no promising way.

However, these methods are not suitable at all, but the misbelief that it is the right way is deeply rooted, starting with the purchase over the management up to marketing.

Because if they would accept or accept the fact that projects are unsuitable, then they would also have to completely rethink their way of working and thinking for the most part. Experience has shown that this is not easy.

With this book I try to give you the right momentum to overcome this hurdle.

unique selling point

Agile and waterfall methods are generally compared only in the area of project management and implementation. This is done quickly, but neither helpful nor useful.

In order to be able to work agile, for example, the process must be started in the idea phase and the entire company and possible service providers must think agile and act agile to a large extent. And this also applies to areas of the company that you may not have even thought of, such as purchasing, human resources or marketing.

Therefore, I deal with the topic holistically from the management, the stakeholders over the marketing and of course the implementation teams up to the purchase and show why most comparisons are misleading and one must fail with projects in the digitization.

iterations

This book is subject to constant change. I regularly incorporate new experiences and feedback from readers and customers into the new editions.

In the meantime, the number of pages has almost doubled within a few weeks. There were only very small changes in the last iterations.[1]

---

[1] https://en.wikipedia.org/wiki/Scrum_Sprint

table of contents

Digitalization

Digitization does not only take place in the depths of an IT department. The advancing digitalization is rather a fundamental and profound change of behavior patterns.

Digitalization is as disruptive as the machine revolution. Not only does it change media use and information consumption, it simply changes everything.

My kids look at me questioningly when I talk about phoning. You send voice messages via WhatsApp. It's terrible for me, but it's her new environment. You are used to communicating asynchronously with several people at the same time. This is only possible thanks to the ongoing digitalization process.

All information is available to us virtually always and at any time. Consumers are completely differently positioned and enlightened.

No B2B dealer today still needs who-supplies-what. Mail order companies that do not ship the goods on the same day and inform the consumer about every step of the delivery process are no longer sustainable for some consumers today.

Certain product ranges, such as toys, are almost completely shifted into the digital universe.

Digitization is taking place at home at an even faster pace. More and more consumers use Netflix, Amazon Prime and Co. like normal television, in my circle of acquaintances many already use a Google Assistant, Amazon Alexa or a Philips HUE light control.

With Apple Pay, all I need is my face to pay and I no longer must remember or enter all my PINs.

This completely normal use of digital services in the private sphere means that customers also expect this simple service from companies. And that's exactly what they said 10 years ago: a B2B application only must be functional. A few cryptic commands were part of it at that time, but today one expects in the B2B environment as well as in the B2C environment individualized, optimized and positive user experiences.

If I want to adapt and prepare myself as an entrepreneur or manager for the requirements of digitization, I must adapt my mentality, my mindset, my attitude to it. I must be open and curious, and I have to be totally committed to change. It is not very helpful to gloss over the current state and fool yourself or others.

In the context of digitalization, this is often referred to as disruption. Derived from the Latin disrumpere = destroy or smash, it means that existing, familiar and often long-standing business processes and behaviors are radically questioned and replaced. You can decide to take part or better still to be a pioneer or to perish.

As an entrepreneur, you are not only well advised to approach your company, your products or services and the traditional processes as openly, curiously and critically as possible. Information and advice from your own industry associations or experts are usually well-intentioned, but should at least be viewed with the utmost caution, not to say neglect.

Disruptive innovations and truly new business models often come from outside the industry. Outsiders do not adhere to existing conventions and question the learned thinking patterns and frameworks that have been accepted within their own industry for years.

In order to experience the future, you must be prepared to bring your own traditional and functioning business model into difficulties through new innovations.

You need the willingness to kill your current business model with your new one!

Because one thing is certain: If you don't do it, someone else will! And it's hard to recover from.

Let's take the furniture industry as an example. Here in NRW we have many quite large furniture chains. What they all have in common is that they mainly sell through the large furniture shop. They have optimized this over the last few decades and incentivized their salespeople to do so.

The shop assistant is thus indirectly involved in every sale in the shop. How great is his motivation to point out the internet offer?

What about the delivery times? 6 weeks 3 months. And shortly before the delivery date this is postponed again by 2 weeks. It's just not up to date anymore. Other solutions are needed here. Not everyone has to become IKEA, but if you don't fundamentally change your business model, I promise that you won't live to see it again as a company in 2030.

Look at the number 2 in Europe in the furniture trade, the Steinhoff Group. Yes, there was corruption. But the stock valuation of 6 cents per share today, September 2019, shows where the industry stands.

And this is just one example; the same applies to automotive suppliers, bakers, retailers, garages, painters, hairdressers, doctors in short, for all areas of life and industries.

So, digitalization concerns us all.

digitalization projects

In the beginning there is the idea. And already here the spirits divide often. Some are given the opportunity to lead a digitalization project to success with a high probability, while others fail to define where they stand with the idea and which scenarios lead to success.

Today, digitalization is an area that permeates all areas of a company and it is only a matter of time before all areas will be affected.

Roughly speaking, such digitalization projects are wrongly divided into the following groups:

- project plans
- product development
- production
- services

glossary

- **Project** A project is a unique project with a clear content and a clear start and end time as well as defined resources.

- **Product**
  A product is a produced good or service.

- **Production** You already have experience with at least the 1st product or project and you want to duplicate it.

- **Service**
  Such services are for example Managed Service, Maintenance, Support, Customer Service or similar.

In the following chapters I will go into these different forms of digitization projects and show you which traps await you there and why some of these common descriptions no longer have a place in the digitized world.

A project

The definition of a project according to **DIN 69901**[2]: A *project* is a project which is essentially characterized by the uniqueness of the conditions in their entirety, such as e.g. objectives, time, financial, personnel or other conditions, differentiation from other projects and project-specific organization.

This would make a procedure based on the waterfall model exactly the right one. However, these are exclusively digital projects. Therefore, the answer is a bit more difficult, because programming is a creative process and therefore not really predictable.

---

[2] https://www2.hhu.de/muendlichkeit/Projekt-Netz/DIN.htm

When I manufacture a machine, for example, I usually know all the parameters such as the metal price and the set-up and production times for all the work steps. These usually deviate only minimally. With these parameters I can draw up an accurate waterfall type plan with milestones, a start date and a planned end date as well as an accurate personnel plan and all costs.

However, projects in the digital age are many times more complex. On the one hand, there is usually a multitude of different ways to the goal and on the other hand, there is usually a sheer infinite number of variables that are hardly manageable and can never be completely grasped.

Let's say you want to build an interactive interface for your customers. The information is derived from CRM (Customer Relationship Management), PIM (Product Information Management) and your FIBU (Financial Accounting).

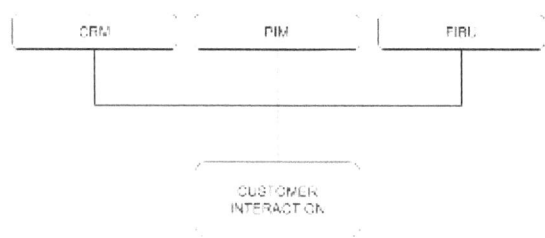

The admittedly very simplified assumption could be: I build a view that simply aggregates and displays the data from all systems.

This doesn't seem like witchcraft. I simply take a ready-made tool like a simple ESB (Enterprise Service Bus), which specializes in reconciling data from different data sources. With another display tool, such as a FAAS (Frontend-as-a-Service), I then display the data, done!

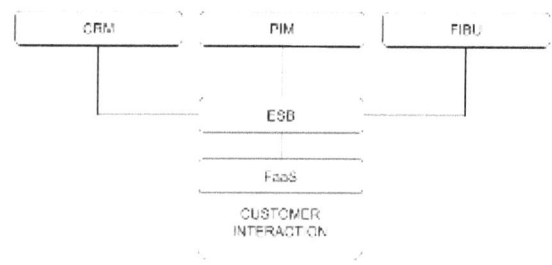

Or as a simple calculation example:

CRM + PIM + FIBU + ESB + FAAS = Project

Let us also assume that each of the interfaces is described exactly before the start of the project and that we can use it to draw up a theoretical architectural plan.

So, this would actually be a very clear waterfall candidate.

Unfortunately, the world of theorists does not always coincide with the real world. In the field of digitalization projects, the average percentage is only 16%. More on that later.

This is what happens: Unfortunately, the assumptions do not apply because, as I said before, creative activities cannot be predicted correctly. In some areas one has experience and knows that in the previously established equation, for example, it is not regulated how the customer authenticates himself, i.e. how it is ensured that the customer only sees his own data and not that of another customer aggregated.

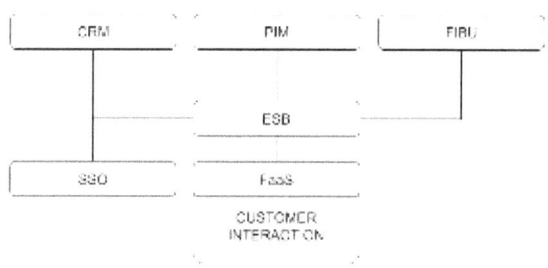

One could conclude from this that we would now simply have to add an SSO (Single Sign-on) to the formula:

CRM + PIM + FIBU + ESB + FAAS + SSO = Project

Rather, however, it is the case that all these components have a complexity of their own and that complexity is multiplied by the addition of another element, since each of the individual elements interacts with each other or with at least one other element.

Therefore, the calculation would rather be as follows:

CRM * PIM * FIBU * ESB * FAAS * SSO = Project

If you now use this model to plan your resources and set the end date as needed for a project, you would be statistically wrong with a probability of over 84%.

In such an enlightened and digitized world, you might ask yourself, how can that be?

Humans can usually only record unstructured quantities up to a number of 6. However, since there are no such small projects or subtasks in a project, the assumptions become more and more inaccurate, the larger the numbers become. Some of them make do with crutches like structuring in groups of 5. With this you can imagine 5, 10, 20, 40, 80, 160. Or 5, 10, 25, 50, 100, 500, 1000. But whether a 64 or 78 is the right one, nobody can say that exactly anymore. Imagine, these abstract numbers now would be person-days effort? You would have 10 milestones, estimated at 64 to 78 person days each. In the end, you would have a possible deviation of 780 - 640 = 140 person days, i.e. approx. 20% deviation from the best case. You can count on that. We forget, however, that we cannot capture such large numbers well. It could also be a 50- 100 or a 40- 80. We just don't know for sure.

Programming is a creative process in which individuals with different knowledge and proposed solutions from their world of experience try to solve the tasks.

In order to present the whole thing even more vividly and mathematically, the[3] faculty could be used as a mathematical description of the complexity.

In short, the faculty describes all the possibilities of combination with each other. For example, there are

263,130,836,933,693,530,167,218,012,160,000.000

(two hundred sixty-three quintilliards one hundred thirty three quintillions eight hundred thirty six quadrillions nine hundred thirty three quadrillions six hundred ninety three trillions five hundred thirty trillions one hundred sixt seven trillion two hundred eighteen trillion

---

[3] In mathematics, the faculty is a function that assigns to a natural number the product of all natural numbers less than and equal to this number. It is abbreviated by an exclamation mark after the argument.

29

twelve billion one hundred sixty million) Possibilities of mixing a 32-card skat game.

Already with 3 cards there are 6 variants to shuffle the cards and with 6 cards there are already 720. Take our example from before, where there were 6 components: 5! = If we now add a component, as in the example SSO, the complexity is not linear: 6!=720. And this is exactly where our problem lies, such a multitude of possibilities, even if you can exclude a multitude of possibilities, you will never really understand them.

For software projects, you cannot meet all of the above requirements to set up a real project. You just have too many unknowns.

As described before, you can certainly exclude one or the other unknown in reality. Let's take our previous example and assume that 2 to 3 components are already working together successfully. This reduces the complexity, the statement and the exponential behavior remains. And note, this is a very simplified view. In reality, an interface already consists of dozens or even hundreds of components. And according to Murphy's law,[4] exactly the three channels with exactly the three data that you need for your project are not used yet and it is possibly unclear whether this is as easy as possible. It's better to just not know at this point.

You see, no matter how you turn and turn it: Projects are unsuitable for software digitization editions.

I know that this simple truth sounds too pessimistic and is often ignored because of this fact.

---

[4] https://de.wikipedia.org/wiki/Murphys_Gesetz

However, as early as the 1960s, computer scientists proclaimed the great [5]software crisis, which continues today.

The Standish Group has been publishing the CHAOS Report for[6]years. Year after year, it examines software projects for their implementation success. In the last version before me, therefore, only 16% of all projects were successfully completed and 84% not.

No matter how big or small these projects were and no matter how experienced the participants were. The value has been fluctuating for years around the Pareto numbers[7] 20/80.

---

[5] https://de.wikipedia.org/wiki/Softwarekrise
[6] https://www.standishgroup.com/store/services/10-chaos-report-decision-latency-theory-2018-package.html
[7] https://de.wikipedia.org/wiki/Paretoprinzip

Incidentally, only 4% of all projects were more successful than planned. So, either the scope was larger, the time was not needed or the quality was better than expected with all other parameters within expectations.

So, it's more like a bet[8] than a good plan. By the way, companies that belonged to this 4% in the past were never able to repeat it in the following year.

In the early 90s, many companies were still in the business of firing nobody because they ordered network hardware from Cisco or software from IBM and something went wrong.

Today, however, software giants that do not follow the API-first approach, such as Microsoft

---

[8] https://firestarter.business/factsheet-software-wasserfallprojekte/

or SAP, can simply no longer meet the rapidly changing requirements. Billions have already been thrown into the sand and entire companies such as Liqui Moly from Ulm, who lost at least a third of their profits through the never-ending switch to Dynamics AX from Microsoft, Otto, Deutsche Bank, Lidl, Edeka, Deutsche Post, Doc Morris and countless more.

What they all have in common is to ignore what Otto summed up briefly after the failure, namely that it is "too complex" for a project. That's not the exception, it's the rule. In our VUCA[9] world, the great time of projects in the digital environment is finally over!

---

[9] https://de.wikipedia.org/wiki/VUCA

bottom line

Implementing digitization projects as projects represents an immense and hardly calculable risk. You should accept the facts and not implement your project as a project! I know that this conclusion is very unpopular and calls for various experts who will find great arguments to hide the truth.

There are other ways to implement his project without the destructive framework of a project, just read the other chapters.

In my book "Cost Estimation in Digital Projects[10]" I go into even more detail about the complex interrelationships in estimating digital projects. And in my free fact sheet: "Software Waterfall

---

[10] https://amzn.to/2AqZX8V

Projects[11]" I summarize the knowledge about digitization projects in a compact way, if you want to learn more about it.

However, projects are well suited if I can control all framework parameters, for example in mechanical engineering or house construction, but not if they become too complex like Stuttgart 21, BER, Elbphilharmonie, ...

---

[11] https://firestarter.business/factsheet:-software-wasserfallprojekte/

No wonder costs are skyrocketing here. But here, too, politicians are demanding the same as some corporate bosses:

We have an idea and expect a fixed price and a date when everything is ready. This also works for small things and only needs to be scaled up.

But right here, as we've learned, you're wrong about everything.

There would also be an easy way here to approach a real corridor. With the knowledge of the maximum deviation applied in projects of Hochtief, Bilfinger, etc. for the public sector and the average deviation from the mean value, it is possible to calculate a corridor of probability, which the statements apply, if one puts the complexity into relation and by the so-called Monte Carlo simulation.

For digitalization projects I provide a finished template of the "Monte Carlo Simulation[12]" free of charge.

I once took the liberty of calculating this for the BER[13] ;-). Of course, I do not have all the facts available, as the public sector has, but it is enough for a forecast: The probability that the BER 2021 will go into operation is with my calculations about 25%. In 2025, the probability will already be 50%, but we will not find a 95% probability until 2028. This means that the airport is only likely to go into operation 5% after 2028. So, if you are planning a flight from or to Berlin in 2029, you can really use the BER.

ways out

---

[12] https://firestarter.business/portfolio/monte-carlo-simulation/
[13] Airport Berlin Brandenburg

Of course, there are other possibilities besides the pure coincidence that a project can be finished in time/budget/quality. Or I could just burden my employees with countless unpaid overtime hours. However, since we currently have an employee market in the digitalization industry, this is certainly not very popular.

I can also commission a service provider with the implementation and, as it were, pass the implementation risk on to them by contract.

An experienced service provider knows the risks of course and would try to include this risk in his offer. But he cannot calculate all risks 100%, because otherwise he would not be marketable with his price.

This is where overtime, nearshoring or offshoring occurs at the service provider. But what often suffers is the quality. And such projects also often end up in court. None of that would be necessary.

"One" product

The definitions of a software product according to **ISO/IEC Standard 24765 are as** follows:

The current ISO/IEC standard 24765 replaces DIN standard 44300 and contains the following definitions for software.

- Software is a program or set of programs designed to run a computer.
- Software are programs and the associated documentation.
- Software are programs and, if applicable, the associated documentation and other data that are necessary for the operation of a computer.

As you can see, the definitions date back to over 20 years ago. Today we are probably talking more about apps (applications) with this definition. What is important for us, however, is what we understand by a digital product today. Many years ago, we had already detached ourselves from the computer. First attempts by Apple in 1993 with the Newton[14] and later in 1996 with the Palm Pilot, which in[15]contrast to the Newton was really usable, launched the mobile age.

---

[14] https://de.wikipedia.org/wiki/Newton_(PDA)
[15] https://de.wikipedia.org/wiki/Palm_Pilot

In 2007, Apple also heralded mass suitability with the iPhone. I actually only joined Apple in 2008, because in 2007 I was still a Blackberry disciple.

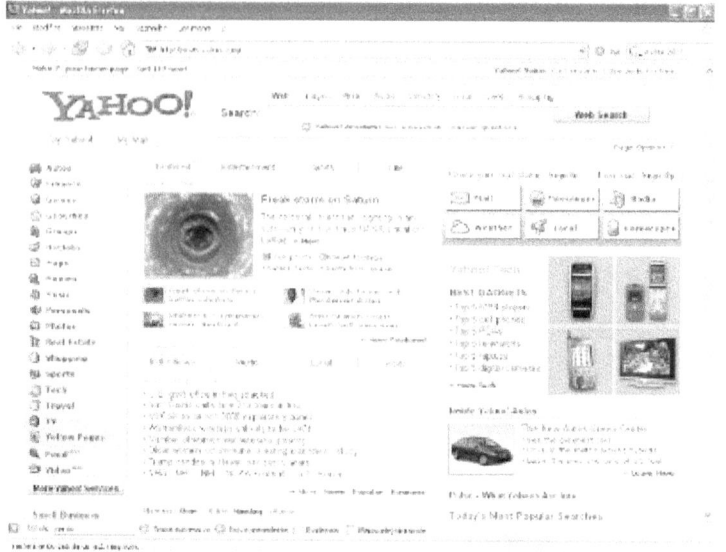

At the same time, GMX was founded in 1996 as a portal and mail service. In the beginning, applications that ran successfully in the browser, portals such as Yahoo, were the first social networks such as Facebook to come onto the market in 2004. Internet shops, intranets and the like also changed our view of digital products.

Today, a digital product can be a voice application on an Amazon Alexa assistant, an application on a wearable[16], such as a watch or a digital T-shirt, a SmartHome thermostat or a lamp.

16 https://de.wikipedia.org/wiki/Wearable_Computing

An all-encompassing definition is therefore difficult. I'll try this one:

A digital product is an application that interacts with other digital applications or a user.

This can be a digital display in a supermarket, an app that optimizes maintenance intervals for a machine or a web application that helps with a healthy diet.

In the headline I deliberately put the "on" in quotation marks. This is because it is exclusively a question of bringing "a" new product onto the market or improving an existing product. If there is already a finished prototype that is to be duplicated and therefore is more about rationalization and improvement of the process, then the following chapters are more goal-oriented for you.

Arriving here, the question arises, why didn't you choose **a project**?

If you already know why a digital product should not be realized in a project, you can simply read on.

To all others I recommend reading the chapter **Project** now and then return here.

The following paragraphs deal with the intention to create a completely new product, to revise an old one or to add new features. The latter could be an exception on a case-by-case basis.

Let's start at the beginning: It is difficult for us to really put ourselves in other people's shoes as well as in the shoes of our target group.

Sometimes there is such a thing as a plumber who develops a plumbing app for plumbers and can put himself in the position of a large number of potential customers. But I often know the case where a sanitary manufacturer believes from customer surveys that he knows what his customers want and builds an app that incorporates all customer wishes. However, most of these apps fail or at least do not manage to have the hoped-for added value, but to destroy huge amounts of money beforehand. Marketing has even developed personas and empathy maps for this purpose to develop stereotypical images of the target group and to make them transparent and visible.

Nevertheless, we continue to develop products that simply won't ignite.

I have put together some links with further information for you:

- https://www.scrum-academy.de/product-owner/wissen/gescheiterte-produkte/

- https://startup-helpers.de/insights/startup-scheitern-produktidee-vs-idee/

- https://www.springerprofessional.de/produktmanagement/produkteinfuehrung/woran-produkteinfuehrungen-scheitern/6597650

- https://de.slideshare.net/MeandCompany/warum-innovationen-scheitern-11-20141209

Yeah, but your idea is the best, right?

Look, even really big, innovative and successful companies like Heinz have been successfully producing ketchup since 1876. Surveys showed that many wanted a green ketchup. That was the right thing to do. But do we know what we want? Have we thought about what the ketchup on a bratwurst looks like? And had we thought that ignorant people would probably make funny comments if we put such a sauce on the fries?

McDonald's also tried to **target** adults. 300
million dollars were invested in market research
in 1996. The result: the burger "Arch Deluxe".
This was advertised with an advertising clip in

which children were disgusted and their faces twisted as they were presented with a burger of adult taste. Parents were obviously not willing to dig deeper into their pockets for the deluxe burger, so the product was taken out of the assortment after about a year.

Men need men's pencils; women need women's pencils - right? Since 2011, the French company BIC has been able to answer this with a clear "no". Because the "bic for her" caused a proper shitstorm for the company. Women probably don't need a pencil, which in glittering pastel colors lies particularly comfortably in women's hands.

There are countless such products, I already mentioned the Apple Newton.

What can we learn from this?

1. At the right time, in the right place: Sometimes happiness is also part of it.

2. Knows your target group: gender-specific doesn't always fit.

3. Market research is not always right (My tip: the C.L.U.B method[17]).

4. Sometimes just common sense helps.

5. Failure doesn't mean you can't succeed.

Is that enough for you or have you never wondered that the election prognoses are sometimes so wrong?

---

[17] https://firestarter.business/portfolio/c-l-u-b-methode/

But how can you still act successfully if these conventional methods do not necessarily lead to the goal in the rapidly changing digital world?

You can find the answer here in the summary.

So, if you want to develop a product and you have an idea for it, all you have to do is minimize the risk of failure, learn quickly and roll out what you have learned immediately with minimal risk. The whole thing can also be called Lean Startup and C.L.U.B.[18] is the suitable method for it, which I will explain later on.

Take the safe route and do not place a project bet whose outcome you cannot predict. Waterfall projects are therefore practically excluded here.

Unless you already have a good product and want to add a feature that the well-managed community wants and persistently justifies.

---

[18] https://firestarter.business/portfolio/c-l-u-b-methode/

If it's even a small feature. Then you can also use the waterfall as a method if necessary.

In any case, you should not ignore the community, but rather deal with it more intensively and also outside of surveys!

production

As in the previous chapters, the focus here is exclusively on digital products and not on industrial or handcrafted products.

I assume that it is a finished successful product, which is mainly about an optimization of the production or sales process and not about a further development or new development, because then the other chapters would be more informative.

First of all, we should distinguish whether it is a combination product consisting of software and hardware such as a Smartwatch or a maintenance sensor on a machine or pure software.

Let's start with the **combination products**. On the one hand, we differentiate between products for trade, industry and products that are not typical consumer goods. A digital thermostat is just as much a part of this as a heart rate monitor from the medical sector, but a heart rate monitor for the wrist in sports is not. This is assigned to typical consumer goods. When it comes to consumer goods, customers and markets react differently and behave completely differently.

Let's take a look at a company like Würth[19], for example. We have succeeded in completely integrating entire customer groups into the "Würth System" in such a way that it is very difficult for customers to buy products from other manufacturers in the future and is also superfluous. Companies such as Phillips have

[19] https://www.wuerth.de/

also managed to establish their own digital HUE[20] world in the field of lamps.

In markets in which the rule applies, the further away from consumption the better, combination products or proprietary hardware platforms can still be established today. So here you can confidently proceed with your ideas. I recommend the KanBan method for process control. Since time does not stand still, I recommend you read the chapter *Ideas*.

Let us now look at combination products that are pure consumer goods. Here I certainly make myself unpopular again, with one or the other future and fact denierer.

---

[20] https://www2.meethue.com/de-de

Because we have a fundamental problem here: customers are becoming less and less [21]loyal to the brand. And outside of Germany, the brand is already no longer as important today as it is in Germany itself.

The customer is increasingly concerned only with function, design and price and less with the brand.

And where do these products find young customers? To Aliexpress, Wish and Co.!

My children go to the eighth grade of a grammar school in a small town in North Rhine-Westphalia. Your classmates and their parents

21

https://www.wuv.de/marketing/markentreue_der_deutschen_nimmt_ab

https://www.springerprofessional.de/vertriebskanaele/unternehmen---institutionen/junge-kunden-sind-weniger-markentreu/16331548 are increasingly shopping online at the above platforms. Because the goods offered there are getting better and better and also the delivery times are getting shorter and shorter. Similar headphones like the Apple Air Pods are available in very good quality starting at 19 Euro instead of 249 Euro. Cheap start already at 4,95 incl. shipping costs.

Here in Spain, where I'm working on this book on holiday, you can find at fnac a big French chain similar to the Media Markt in Germany, these products in the display right next to the Apple products and on pallets.

What does that mean for us? To arrive against the superiority of the Chinese is hardly possible at the moment and we are still before the right start of the Asians, that will simply not work and if the Asians really get started, they are years ahead of us.

Do you know the brand xiaomi[22]? Google once after. They offer eScouters with apps, first-class smartphones that outshine many Samsung devices and are very, very cheap and good. In a few years these brands will have displaced many other well-known brands.

So, what can you do to still be successful?

Cooperating is one way. Hardware from Asia is just unbeatable good and cheap. In 2019, however, they are still designing the software there according to Asian models, and this is mainly shrill and colorful and still often prone to errors with not yet so good customer experiences. So, this is a great opportunity to score for you.

---

[22] https://www.mi.com/global/

When it comes to innovative software, I strongly recommend that you read the *Ideas* chapter.

I would not develop hardware in this area myself for the future, but with Asian partners. If you would like to develop hardware for this area yourself, then I can also recommend the Ideas chapter after the following paragraph.

Let's take a look at the **software now**. As described before, this is not about new software, but about improving the distribution.

First and foremost, let us deal with the distribution possibilities. Here, too, we distinguish between consumer goods and all other products.

Let's start with non-original consumer goods. In contrast to the hardware before, there is the possibility here to drive a two-pronged strategy. It makes sense to win a clientele through hardware and software combinations, but it can also make sense to offer your hardware platform to other providers or to establish a software platform. So, you reach more range quickly and minimize your own risk. In this combination certainly one of the greatest opportunities for German SMEs to benefit from digitization, whether as a machine manufacturer or semi-finished product manufacturer. Therefore, you should intensively deal with the topics around the platform economy. The article: "How platforms determine the digital economy[23]" from Computerwoche 2019 can be a good introduction for you.

---

[23] https://www.computerwoche.de/a/wie-plattformen-die-digitalwirtschaft-bestimmen,3547305

How do you market your software now? In the past, this was done on a floppy disk, CD-ROM, download, etc.

But these distribution channels are all outdated. Today there are mainly three common ways:

1. Distribute an app via a platform such as Google Playstore, Apple, Microsoft, etc..

2. A web app (progressive web app); an application that runs in a browser and behaves similarly to a native application.

3. Offer your own software and/or hardware platform such as CCU2 for home automation or Schüttflix for bulk solids.

In the first two ways, the distribution is so simple and automated that you only have to take care of marketing or improve your product. In the third case, the path is already more complex and must certainly first be newly developed. So, read on in the *Ideas* chapter.

In the area of software as a consumer good it is a bit more limited. Here there are mainly two distribution channels:

1. Distribute an app via a platform such as Google Playstore, Apple, Microsoft, etc..

2. A web app, i.e. an application that runs in a browser and behaves similarly to a native application.

Here I always recommend both ways. This way there is no dependency and the revenue does not have to be shared with the web app.

Here, too, it is more a question of constantly improving the product.

You will find the right solution for the maintenance and operation of these solutions in the chapter *Service.*

bottom line

Times have changed. Today, the distribution of software is largely automated and is greatly simplified by existing software platforms. It's more about rolling out good marketing and constantly improving the product than about working on technical distribution. Unless you want to start your own platform.

service

The operation of a service is usually divided into three areas: the recurring tasks for the operation of digital products, the reading and cleaning of log files and the importing of patches, etc. The service is usually provided in the form of a service. It is precisely this operation that is increasingly being automated on platforms such as Amazon's aws in so-called managed Cubernet[24] clusters.

Nevertheless, the maintenance of the application remains, even if the environment can and should be automated as far as possible today.

---

[24] https://kubernetes.io/de/docs/tutorials/kubernetes-basics/create-cluster/

But this, too, is currently changing. Take Salesforce, for example. You can develop an application for the Salesforce universe and then only have to develop it further and are not responsible for its operation. Such performances can best be optimized and controlled with the KanBan method developed by Toyota.

The second area is customer service. On the one hand, this is about helping users, on the other hand it is about correcting errors and adhering to service level agreements, so-called SLAs.

This includes, for example, the times when the service offered is not available, restoration of a condition or reaction times after an error.

This is where KanBan comes in again to provide an ideal environment to keep these service promises. In addition, one should not neglect the LEAN idea, because there is a huge potential slumbering here. The Kanrum method, for example, ensures that user objections, system failures and errors found contribute to the sustainable improvement of the product, the optimization of the process and the avoidance of errors in the future.

For me, the third area is more a product than a service. Here we are talking about service applications such as Wunderlist[25] or Trello[26]that help you to organize yourself, Vermietet.de[27] a service for landlords, IFTTT[28] an automation

---

[25] https://www.wunderlist.com
[26] https://trello.com/de
[27] https://www.vermietet.de/
[28] https://ifttt.com/

service or dCommerce.blog[29] a blog about digitization in retail.

The operation and support of these applications and products is certainly in the right place here, but the adaptation and further development I would handle in any case with the involvement of the KanBan teams deployed here in another team with a different budget.

---

[29] https://dcommerce.blog/

There is an ideal method for the support and operation of software: Kanban and its extension Kanrum. More about this in the appendix. It should be noted here that the pure operation of the further development must be differentiated but must be in a lively exchange.

Ideas and ways out

Either you have jumped directly here, because you are still at the very beginning of your idea or you know now after reading the other chapters, that it is presumptuous and mostly wrong to believe, one already knows the ideal finished product.

"Because only the fact that you develop a project from which you cannot yet determine in detail how to achieve success will ultimately produce the desired result.

Donald G. Reinertsen, 2009

I have seen this quote from Donald, who is considered one of the pioneers of the Lean Startup[30] method, on several stages. And most

30 https://en.wikipedia.org/wiki/Lean_startup

of the time it was relativized again immediately. It's a pretty strong statement and obviously an open slap in the face for one or the other. He is talking about the fact that preliminary planning is not possible. I can only agree with him and no project without planning.

So far, we have collected enough arguments and evidence to clearly support this statement.

Now that we have said goodbye to the methods of the predigital world, we can devote ourselves to the actual purpose of this book.

The original title should be "Agile vs. Waterfall". But that would not have done justice to the content of this book at all.

Because it's not just about the method and the mindset. It's also about realizing you'll never finish. Anyone who thinks that they have developed the ultimate product, the best platform or the best service today will be outdated tomorrow and will soon be left behind by more innovative and faster acting companies.

Instead of thinking in small budgets, we must think more innovatively and constructively.

Let's take an example from the digital pioneers and industry giants in the US like Google, Apple, Facebook and Amazon who spend billions on research and innovation.

Successful companies usually spend well over 10% of their expenses on a desirable tomorrow and a large proportion on cannibalising their current business model.

In Germany, on the other hand, the share is far too low, averaging 3.5%[31] of expenditure. Even if there are exceptions in Germany in 2019 such as the VW Group, which is struggling to survive after all the scandals and the completely sleepy trends in Europe and Asia.

For the largest market in Japan (40 %), for example, VW has not brought a single vehicle onto the market for the so-called Kei-Cars,[32] or even one in the planning stage.

I would therefore rather recommend doubling the third largest budget[33] after Amazon and

---

[31] https://www.deutschlandinzahlen.de/tab/deutschland/wissenschaft forschung/forschung-und-entwicklung/innovationsaufwendungen-anteile-am-umsatz

[32] https://de.wikipedia.org/wiki/Kei-Car

[33] https://t3n.de/news/ausgaben-fuer-forschung-volkswagen-auf-platz-3-hinter-amazon-und-google-1121805/

Google to make up for all the omissions of the last 20 years. Have you ever connected to your iPhone in a Tesla? Great, isn't it? Compare that with the Apple-Car-Play from VW that still needs a cable connection to work, despite the wireless charging process.

Here, too, VW has not heeded my book title "Digitalization is not a project" and will not bring any improvements to the market in 2020 either.

Yes, I know the details that make it difficult to technically improve access. But why don't you think differently instead of simply installing a docking station for Apple and Android on the already mostly useless factory navigation systems and controlling the navigation, radio and Co. directly with an app from the smartphone? This could be done by delivering the smartphone directly and establishing a platform for third-party extension providers. But there are certainly more and better ideas. When do we implement them?

And there is still more to digitization. Is it still acceptable today that VW cars are only designed for a maximum of 10 years? Let's take a look at the EOS. For example, we hardly find any cars older than 10 years. And this is no exception. But where is the market pointing today? I'm renting a car or at least part of a car. The breakthrough for eMobility finally came in Germany in 2019. But VW gives the guarantee for the battery and thus the expected life span with only 8 years.

Consumers are no longer able to keep up with these ever faster cycles and many are already switching to car sharing models[34] from Daimler, BMW or Sixt. In the future, we will no longer buy ourselves in the quantities of cars and also no longer in the short cycles that the advertising world wants to talk us into. When I leave the office in Cologne, it's usually only a few seconds until I'm sitting around the corner in a convertible and can drive off immediately by app for little money. Then why buy a convertible? There's one of these all over the place and it's getting more and more? Does VW already build cars for this purpose? Do you already adapt the cool and even simpler apps of the eScouter? Or will the Amarok diesel continue to be built with a soot particle filter?

---

34 https://www.tagesschau.de/wirtschaft/carsharing-111.html

Don't take this as a VW Bashing, but as a wake-up call. These or similar signs apply to every industry.

Let's take an example that I find again and again in my own professional life. A customer thinks my shop is outdated; I need a new one. The new one should be based on a current technology, otherwise with the processes like the old one only run in nice.

Notice anything yet? What the fuck are you doing? I cannot rule out the possibility that at some point the technology will have to be replaced because it poses security risks, or the performance is inadequate. That's perfectly okay, too. But let's be honest, in very few cases you sell more afterwards. Rather, instead of such a mammoth project, you should make your shop a little better every day for customers. To do everything that pays off, so that the customer experience becomes better and better. Already in 2017 I wrote an article in my blog http://dCommerce.blog with the title "An eCommerce Shop-Relaunch is so yesterday[35]".

Let's get back to the trials: There are different methods for different complex tasks.

The overview is very simple:

---

[35] https://dcommerce.blog/ein-ecommerce-shop-relaunch-ist-so-gestrig/

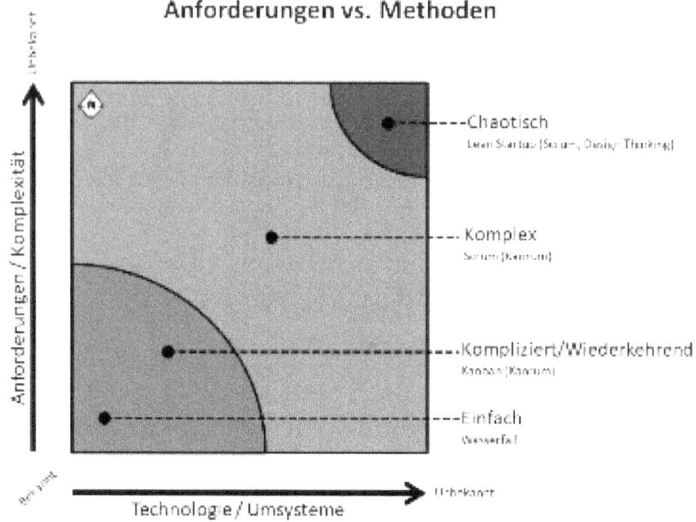

Anforderungen vs. Methoden

The more complex and unpredictable, the less suitable the waterfall method is as a project approach. Thus, all PRINCE2 and PMI and other experts from the predigital era are unfortunately not qualified to lead you into the digital future, because digital projects hardly ever fall into the realm of easy. And even for a service or operation of such is as previously described Kanrum the means of choice.

But these are the experts at the big consulting companies or most agencies or people with a super degree but without real experience and without experience you are often tempted to follow some theories or alleged best practices that are often more than glossed over. Here it needs real experience and no observers and theorists.

But why do I think I can present myself here as someone who can offer solutions to the dilemma?

A short excursion into my biography is allowed here, but you may skip it confidently.

>>

At the end of the 80s, I learned Refa techniques in mechanical engineering, when Refa[36]technici

87

ans walked through the company with the stopwatch and noted exactly how long each individual work step takes and calculated from it exact plans for the effort of the next machine, even if it always deviated a little from the previous one. After that, in the early 90s, I was in projects aimed at highly customized automated warehouses. Here, heavy machinery construction had to act together with simple software and guarantee that the software would work on the acceptance date. In the middle of the nineties I already managed my first own projects, which were about creating and managing network infrastructure. At the end of the nineties I was then in the hardware development in the area DSL and later WLL on the way and 2001 I developed as a technical leader with my team the first Smartphone for WLL networks: the Mi-Phone. Later followed

---

[36] https://de.wikipedia.org/wiki/Vorgabezeit

the development of an ERP system and a digital cash register in my own company, which I later sold, and I worked as a consultant for the Product Owner at companies like Amazon, eBay, ePages and PayPal. Later I introduced agile techniques as product owner of various products at shopware. Since 2015 I have been CTO at synaigy GmbH in Cologne, one of the leading digital agencies in Germany. I am also involved in various digitalization projects there.

Herewith the excursion into my biography should be also to end. I would like to mention that I have obtained all Scrum certificates and have been awarded as Scrum Professional. At the University of Cologne, I also obtained a certificate for conventional project management according to the waterfall model.

So, I claim to have gotten to know a lot of different projects and project types from the theoretical background as well as from experience and I claim to be able to draw from my profound knowledge and experience with a clear conscience. <<

Let's now come to the procedure for digital projects, which I have adapted, used and continuously developed over the past few years.

It is a model in different phases and depending on how far you are you can also start in one of the following phases or compare the first phases of the procedure with your previous procedure. Above all, however, it is also a never-ending cycle of innovation.

It is not something entirely new, but merely a nesting of individual established procedures, such as Lean Startup[37] or Scrum[38]. Since Scrum is a deliberately incomplete framework and Lean Startup doesn't contain everything a successful digital project needs, I merged them and added the missing building blocks.

Let's start with the idea. The idea is the starting point of every project. This idea can come from yourself, from surveys of potential or existing clients, or from design thinking[39] workshops.

It is important whether this idea also fits into your concept for your company or whether you are willing to subordinate your company to this idea. You should check this first.

---

[37] http://theleanstartup.com/principles
[38] https://www.scrumalliance.org/
[39] https://de.wikipedia.org/wiki/Design_Thinking

Then you can see what this idea really brings to your customers, what advantages it offers your customers and what added value, which USP do[40] you offer?

With the knowledge of your target group and the added value, you now go and see how you can develop a prototype that validates your acceptance with the least possible resources and risk.

This prototype is also called an MVP (Minimum Viable Product) in short: the smallest possible product that creates added value. In addition, the business value of the idea (the potential value of implementation) is assessed from the customer's and company's point of view. This is put in relation to the implementation risk and a clear recommendation for action is given.

---

[40] https://firestarter.business/usp/

Things with high risk and low potential business value should **not be** implemented. A low risk and a high potential business value, on the other hand, is a clear signal of implementation.

On this topic I have written a very detailed book "Agile Project Management: Creating Maximum Business Value: Starting with a Customer-Centric Perspective and Maximizing Value for a Secure Future[41]", where you will learn all the details about the so-called C.L.U.B. method, which describes and prescribes this procedure in detail.

Such an MVP can also simply be a display with the product, for example. Here, for example, you can measure whether potential customers are even willing to click on an ad that may

---

[41] https://amzn.to/31W8bSi

already contain a price. In the aforementioned book there are countless such examples which help to validate his assumption of having thrown a good idea into the race. All MVPs have in common a very low effort and a very low implementation risk.

Once one has validated one's assumption, one develops the next step of evolution. Or if not, you can start a new attempt with small means, without immediately flopping with the full budget on the market.

So, you go into an agile ongoing process of development (called iterations in the Scrum), where there is no big roadmap, because the respective goals a development cycle, which is on average two weeks, is sufficient to create a new measurable value. Above all, you learn exactly what works on the market right now. So, you can continuously improve your product and do not take a big risk.

In addition, you are as flexible as possible and can react to new trends every two weeks.

What you don't have is a fixed project plan or a budget that lasts longer than 4-6 weeks. Because if you don't manage to create a value for the company in 3 development units one after the other that is greater than the effort, then you simply stop! It then makes no sense to pursue the project further, "we don't have a project" that would dictate this.

There are methods that can happen in the event of failure, such as re-evaluating all projects and incorporating what has been learned into the project in order to redesign or expand the idea.

Or you simply get the realization that the idea was simply not good or at least does not fit the target group.

I can hear the alarm bells ringing! Purchasing says if I'm supposed to buy something like this from a service provider, how is that supposed to work?
The managing director doesn't know how high the budget is that he needs, what happens to the unused budget?

What if I produce something completely different than originally assumed, that is not possible in our Group, we have shareholders, how can I explain that?

In the end, these are all excuses to disregard the fact that the world no longer functions like this!

But yes, for some it requires a complete reorientation. Here the purchasing department or the controller, the marketing department must now calculate potential values and recalculate them every few weeks. Yeah, it's different than before. That creates effort in places that did not exist before, that changes the power structure and because it is so strange, it makes you afraid.

However, to deny oneself and thus the current state of science would be highly negligent.

It's a dilemma you can't give in to.

Of course, I also know the voices that say: Agile and Scrum is a lot of folklore with colorful notes or it is seen more like a religion.

And yes, unfortunately, that is partly true.

I know a lot of people who think they know Lean or Scrum from books, or who have even attended a course at Scrum.org and have acquired a Lifetime Certificate in Scrum. But all of them have never experienced that it works and what you can do with it.

Take a look at what shopware, for[42] example, as one of the smallest digital shop providers on the market, is currently doing and what big companies like Adobe are doing with the

---

[42] https://www.shopware.com/

competitor software Magento to make them look old.[43]

In addition, there are very few projects that are really Lean and realized after Scrum. I have already roughly described the framework parameters before and also described what unnecessary discomfort this causes in humans.

All this leads to style blossoms like ScrumBan, agile fixed price, Scrum projects with milestones and deadlines and much more.

That's not the way the world works.

All these projects are therefore more or less doomed to failure, because they are despite all

---

[43] https://magento.com/

the agile painting only predigital projects or even a spectacle. I have already described ways out, which there can be, in the previous chapters.

I hereby appeal to all decision-makers to deal with the facts and to enter the digital age with the right methods.

Every compromise leads to a worse product than would have been possible with the given budget.

Just because the assumption that function X and Y are absolutely necessary, because the largest customer demands it, often leads to the Pareto principle that 80% of the expenses are spent on only 20% of the possible business value. Instead of creating 60 % more value with this 80 %, it might create one that cannot be determined at the beginning of the project.

Previously I had described one of the biggest mistakes in larger companies, which repeatedly leads to problems: The important customer expects this, the interface/software is not able to do so, etc.. What they all have in common is that such statements are not further questioned. If it costs me 100,000 Euros, but the expected return of the customer with an expected life of 8 years is only 90,000 Euros, and I could have created another value with the 100,000 Euros, which extends the expected customer life of all customers by 30% on average, or lets the company win new customers and bring the 200,000 Euros. Then this does not prevent most entrepreneurs from ignoring it or from even looking at it. We like to stick to decisions we've made. This fact is as scientifically proven as it is dangerous. A radical rethink is needed here.

As already shown in the first chapters using various examples, companies sometimes simply don't know what they need or really want and on the other hand these statements from customers can be an extremely helpful warning factor.

They point out that their companies are not competitive for the future and therefore may not be able to survive in the future. You could take such customers, even if they are your biggest today, but they are pushing you into rigid and outdated structures, just let them go or even better take them with you into the 21st century.

Because it is even more dangerous if someone else comes and migrates the customer to his own platform because he was not able to do it himself and they put a lot of effort into it, which is not worth it because the customer uses more modern methods from another provider. Then you have invested and still lose the customer. It also shows in which position you stand with the customer: Are you at eye level with him?

Advise the customer, if not another does this. I know of many such projects in which a supplier bent to integrate a customer into an outdated process, and only a few months or years later another supplier came and offered a service that was lean and modern and made old processes superfluous.

If the in-house software is the limiter, then it is outdated and out of date. Do you still have SAP in use? Have you ever thought about modern systems? Now would be a good time to change. Otherwise this system will slow you down again and again in the future and prevent innovation.

Some people are now thinking: "Of course I want to digitize the supply chain and invest a few hundred thousand euros in it, but my ERP has to stay. *The project would be far too big! Here the tail waggles with the dog.*

But that is nonsense, because during the process there will always be new requirements in real time. Old systems are hardly designed for this. Then you start with compromises ... and then you have your eternal wooden leg that you have to carry around with you. And yes, it is correct, an ERP/CRM is also a digitization project and as such also not suitable as a project. There were already plenty of examples of this too (Otto, Lidl, ...). Do you know Salesforce as CRM? So, you can start small and grow slowly and migrate into iterations, very agile.

Here it doesn't matter whether you develop a product in your company or with an external service provider. The loser in any case is the client. It may well be that others lose in addition, such as the implementation team or the service provider. But even if I disregard this, it is still certain that I, as a client, will obstruct my own path to more profit and success.
No matter how I turn it around, "Digitization is not a project." I hope we're clear.

With methods like Lean Startup, Scrum or the C.L.U.B method developed by me you are in good hands in the digital world. However, traditional project management methods are hardly suitable for this digitized complex world.

Rather, they tend to ensure that the project fails, becomes more expensive than necessary or does not achieve the desired effect.

Now I hope you understand why I'm talking about digitization projects and not projects. The mere fact that a project is finite, but digitization is not finite for the time being, forces you to proceed differently than before. Today, continuous adaptation to ever new framework parameters is required. Instead of investing every few years in a renewal that is usually commissioned too late and is already obsolete by the time it is completed, you should invest a certain proportion (a good value is just over 10% of the expenses) of your company's turnover in continuous renewal and research. This will give you a budget with which you can spend X person days per year with your service provider and/or a team of X people all year round.

Do not unnecessarily regulate your opportunities and chances through projects, even for tricky situations there are always experts who can help you out of the dilemma.

In the appendix I have listed an overview of some of the topics covered here such as Lean Startup, Scrum, KanBan, Kanrum and Scrumban as well as the C.L.U.B. method with further links, which, in addition to this first impulse and overview, give you the right tools to be successful with your digitalization project.

appendix

FACTSHEET's

The Waterfall Project Bet

https://firestarter.business/factsheet-software-wasserfallprojekte/

agile

https://firestarter.business/factsheet-agile/

author

In his eCommerce Blog **https://dCommerce.blog** Dietmar Hölscher (B.Sc.) writes in his spare time about developments in the online trade and dedicates himself among other things to various shop systems. It also reports in detail on agile topics. Dietmar has been a Certified Scrum Professional®, Certified Scrum Product Owner® and Certified Scrum Master® for many years.

Since 1995, he has been monitoring the technical infrastructure and service environment available to online merchants and reporting as an independent observer.

Dietmar Hölscher played a major role in the development of DSL and WLL networks in the 1990s. He was one of the most successful Internet providers in Germany and at the beginning of the new millennium, on behalf of the EU, devoted himself to cross-border broadband Internet, RIPE and the European Internet Exchanges.

As a developer he already designed a first simple "Internet shop" in 1995. At that time, automatically filling forms were already regarded as such. In 2005 he started to make his hobby (cooking) his profession and founded an internationally very successful online shop for molecular cuisine. At that time, he encountered many obstacles which had not yet been solved for small traders. He then developed his own ERP and shipping solution, based on a shop system, and later also a fully-fledged POS system.

Even then, he advised leading shop systems, marketplace operators and payment providers. This later paved the way for him into the management of shopware AG, where he established the Business Development department and was responsible for many product innovations such as bepado, the later shopware connect or shopware easy, the later shopware 6.

After a short excursion as a partner of Adrian Hotz to the eCommerce consultancy he feels very comfortable since 2016 as CTO of synaigy GmbH - one of the leading IBM Watson Commerce, Intershop and shopware agencies in Europe. Synaigy as the eCommerce part of the TimeToAct group (>500 employees in Europe) is an important service provider offering integrated solutions for large manufacturers and retailers from the B2B and B2C market throughout Europe.

In addition to technical consulting and implementation, he also accompanies agile change within the Group and with customers.

Current list of books: https://amzn.to/2U1hhKQ

sources

Pictures/Drawings: Dietmar Hölscher

Author picture

: Dieter Hemsing

Imprint

Dietmar Hölscher

Altes Forsthaus am Blomenesch 3

D-48653 Coesfeld in Westphalia

Germany

firestarter.business

I thank my children Ophelia and Tristan, as well as my wife Nicole, who gave me the time under Spain's sun for this book.